INTERMEDIATE

MORE Quick-Start Lessons for the Elementary Class
From the Writers of John Jacobson's MUSIC EXPRESS

Compiled by Tom Anderson

HAL•LEONARD® CORPORATION

7777 W. BLUEMOUND RD. P.O. BOX 13819 MILWAUKEE, WI 53213

Visit Hal Leonard Online at
www.halleonard.com

Table of Contents

Introduction

The first time I taught at the upper elementary level, I was to teach General Music to fifth and sixth graders. The teacher who had been teaching General Music was going to be the new librarian for the school.

I will always remember setting up my room for the first time. This new librarian had a closet full of manipulatives, recordings, scarves, personal instruments and the experience that went with using those materials, all of which she had cleared out before the first day of school. That left me with a bass xylophone, the box of percussion instruments that always seem to appear no matter where you teach (you know the box – filled with red and blue rhythm sticks), recorders that hadn't been used for at least a decade and a console piano.

Thankfully, I had a supportive administration and the position was only half time. I taught in the morning and then headed home in the afternoon to figure out what I was going to teach the next day. I had no textbooks, recordings, posters or any other resources, so it always felt like I had to "punt" for most of my lessons that first year. I sure could have used a resource like *Music Time: Intermediate*. The songs alone would have assisted me through the school year, whether I used them in class or for concerts, but it is the teaching materials that would have helped the most.

I always like to work with music reading no matter what level I teach. Audrey Snyder's information and sequence in the Music Reading chapter would have worked perfectly for my fifth and sixth graders. There is even a song, "Sing a Song!" that can be used as a culmination of what the students have learned.

Classroom instrument lessons are featured as well. There is lots of flexibility, so even if you have only one bass xylophone and a box full of very-used percussion instruments, the material will work. I'll give you a hint: for fifth and sixth grade, buy pairs of drumsticks that they sell out of a plastic paint bucket at most music stores. They are slightly warped, but older elementary students love to use them in music class.

Partner songs are a great way to introduce singing in parts and with conviction. Several are included here, along with listening maps, assessment activities, creative opportunities and more. Where were they when I faced that empty closet (literally and figuratively), and those fifth and sixth graders lined up to enter the music room? What a help you would have been. Quick-start your lessons with *Music Time*!

Tom Anderson

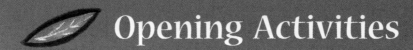

Piano PDF on Enhanced CD

1 Full Performance

2 Accompaniment

Music Rocks!

(4 measures introduction)
Rock (♩ = 126)

**Words and Music by JOHN JACOBSON
and ROGER EMERSON**

1. Mu - sic rocks you when you're up or out!
2. Mu - sic rocks me with a might - y beat!

Mu - sic rocks and I just got - ta shout! Hey!
Mu - sic rocks me from my head to feet! Hey!

Shout

Mu - sic rocks, oh there's one thing I know;
Mu - sic rocks me ev - 'ry day and night!

got my mu - sic so come on let's go! Oh!____
Got my mu - sic and I'm feel - in' right! Oh!____

Yeah!____ Mu - sic rocks! Oh!____

Yeah!____ Mu - sic rocks!

21 *Spoken*

Mu - sic is the mo - tion that will make you hu - man - ize.__

OK TO REPRODUCE

Mel - o - dy and rhy - thm gon - na help you har - mo - nize.

Sing - in' is the thing that's gon - na be there in the end._ Put your

heart in - to your mu - sic and you'll al - ways have a friend!

29 **Build to end**

Sing f

Spoken:
Put your hands together!

Oh!____ Yeah!____ Mu - sic rocks!

Spoken:
Everybody!

Oh!____ Yeah!____ Mu - sic rocks!

37 $f\!f$

Spoken:
One more time!

Oh!____ Yeah!____ Mu - sic rocks!

Oh!____ Yeah!____ Mu - sic rocks!

Teaching Suggestions

- Play the beginning of the accompaniment track (CD Track 2). **ASK: What style of music is this?** (rock)
- Discuss some words that are used for positive comments and encouragement. (cool, awesome, excellent, rocks, rules, etc.)
- Play the beginning of the full performance (CD Track 1). Ask students if they can "name that tune." (Music Rocks!)
- Invite students to sing along with the recording. Even if they only sing the words "music rocks" that will be a good way to introduce the song. Eventually, have them sing and rap all of the lyrics.
- Ask for volunteers to say the spoken phrases towards the end of the song. (Put your hands together!, Everybody!, One more time!)
- Combine singing the song with the choreography that is written above the piano accompaniment (see Enhanced CD).

WEST AFRICAN WELCOME

By Rollo Dilworth

Welcome to Liberia, a West African country that is bordered by Sierra Leone to the northwest, Guinea to the north, and Ivory Coast (Cote D'Iviore) to the east. In Liberia, people commonly greet one another with what is known as a "snapshake." As you finish shaking hands, grasp the middle finger of the other person's hand between your thumb and ring finger, then bring up your hand and release the other person's hand with a snap!

Even though the history of this West African coastal region dates back over 5,000 years, the country of Liberia (meaning "the free land") started out in the early nineteenth century as a United States colony. In the 1820s, a number of freed slaves from the United States crossed the Atlantic Ocean to settle back into their African homeland. In 1847, the Liberian Declaration of Independence was signed. One year later, the Liberian Constitution was ratified and the new republic of Liberia was officially established, becoming the first independent republic on the continent of Africa.

Today there are over three million citizens in Liberia (95% of them are from indigenous African tribes, the other 5% are descendents of former American slaves—called Americo-Liberians). Although English is the country's official language, there are over thirty other languages spoken in Liberia. The Kpelle,

numbering approximately 300,000, is the largest ethnic group in the country.

Like most cultures in Africa, singing, dancing, and performing on instruments play a prominent role in Liberian daily life. Music and dance are used to accompany weddings, welcome celebrations, initiation rituals, religious ceremonies, the birth of a child, the planting of crops, and the harvesting of those crops.

In general, the musical traditions of Africa are dominated by drums and other struck instruments. The types of drums vary in shape, size, function, and timbre. Some of these drums are played with the hand or even the feet, while others are played with a stick. Repetitious rhythmic patterns played by these drums are often layered to create very complex and fascinating textures. The layering of these rhythmic patterns form what is known as a polyrhythm. In addition to indigenous instruments, or those instruments from West Africa, modern musicians in West Africa also use electronic instruments such as guitars and synthesizers.

The clothing of West African culture can be described as "colorful." Similar to the making of a quilt, pieces of cloth are often fashioned into blocks or strips and then combined or layered to form larger pieces of fabric. These larger pieces of fabric are used for creating traditional African fashion. The specific combination of colors and patterns found in African clothing are often used to signify tribal heritage, social status, or even an African proverb.

Since music is an integral part of African life and culture, every citizen is expected to develop basic skills in singing and dancing. One song and dance tradition that is found all over West Africa, including Liberia, is called "Fanga alafia." It is a dance of celebration used to welcome people. The words (in the Yoruba language) are as follows: Fanga alafia, ashé, ashé. "Fanga" means "welcome." "Alafia" means "peace, good will." The word "ashé" means "I agree."

Piano PDF on Enhanced CD

3 Full Performance **4** Accompaniment

Fanga alafia

Traditional West African
Arranged by ROLLO DILWORTH

(5 measures introduction)

mf (sing 1st verse, sing 2nd verse, dance break, sing 1st verse)

1. Fang - a a - la - fi - a a - shé a - shé.
2. Wel - come to ev - 'ry - one with o - pen arms.

Fang - a a - la - fi - a a - shé, a - shé.
Peace, love, good will to you, we're glad you've come.

Fang - a a - la - fi - a a - shé, a - shé.
Wel - come to ev - 'ry - one with o - pen arms.

Fang - a a - la - fi - a a - shé, a - shé.
Peace, love, good will to you, we're glad you've come.

A - shé, a - shé.   A - shé, a - shé.
Wel - come to you.   Wel - come to you.

A - shé, a - shé.   A - shé, a - shé.
Wel - come to you.   Wel - come to you.

OK TO REPRODUCE

Teaching Suggestions

- Discuss various ways of greeting people. (waving, shaking hands, high 5's, etc.)
- Read the first paragraph of the student article, "West African Welcome." Divide into groups of two and practice the "snapshake" greeting. Continue reading and discussing the article.
- Play the full performance (CD Track 3). Invite students to sing along. (pronunciation: *Fahn-ga ah-lah-fee-ah ah-shay ah-shay*)
- Locate the choreography found in the piano accompaniment. Ask for volunteers to perform the movements during the Dance Break as the class sings the song.

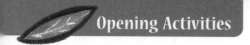

Full Performance   Track Only

A Challenging Warm-Up

By LYNNE CARLSTEIN

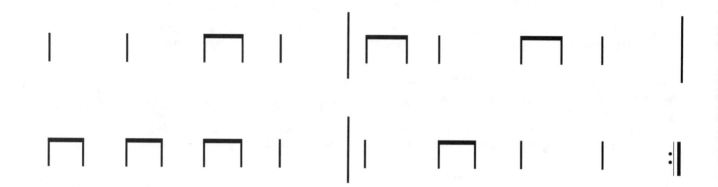

Teaching Suggestions

- Start by stepping the beat. Use the full track (CD Track 5) for accompaniment.
- Clap each measure, students echo. Repeat clapping one measure at a time as students echo. Clap two measures, students echo. Change the response taps (on desks) or pats (on legs).
- Let students take turns leading the class. Use the track only (CD Track 6) for accompaniment.
- Distribute the music or project it on the board (see Enhanced CD). **SAY: When you see one line, you are clapping on the beat. When two lines are combined, you clap twice in the beat.** Repeat the sequence of echo clapping as the students read the music.

7
Full Performance

Play-Along with a Surf Band

(2-measures introduction)
Moderately fast Surf-Rock ($\quarternote$ = 162)

**Instrument Parts by
TOM ANDERSON**

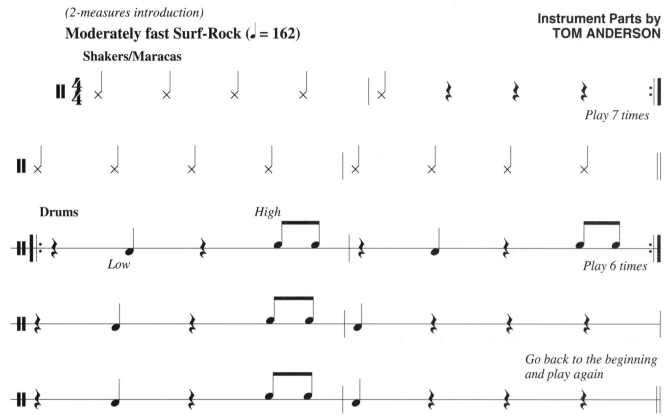

Teaching Suggestions

- Draw a quarter rest on the board. **SAY: When you see this $\quarterrest$, you are to be quiet for one beat. It is called a *quarter rest*.**
- Project "Play-Along with a Surf Band" on the board (see Enhanced CD), or make copies and distribute. **SAY: Musical notes have now replaced the line notation. When the note head is an "X," Shakers and Maracas are played. When the noteheads are filled in, Drums are played.**
- Students playing Drums are to make low and high tones. This is done by playing in the middle of the drum for the low and at the edge for high, or by using bongos and congas where the larger drum is played for the low tone and smaller drum for the high tone.
- Body percussion may be used instead of instruments. Have the students "swish" their hands back and forth using their palms for the Shakers and Maracas part. For the drum part, have students "thump" their chests using an open hand for the bass tone and pat their laps for the high tone.
- Perform the piece using the full performance (CD Track 7).

Begin With the Beat

KEYS TO SIGHT-SINGING SUCCESS

- Create a positive classroom environment. *Be enthusiastic!*
- Either by means of a personal copy or by means of an overhead projector, each student needs to have clear visual access to the reproducible exercises.
- Students will gain the most from this section with consistent practice. Plan to spend at least 3 to 5 minutes on these activities each time the group meets. Regular, consistent practice is optimal.
- Be alert to student successes and sincerely praise students when they do well.
- Don't try to accomplish too much at one time. Learning to sight-read is not an easy task. The goal is *steady, forward progress*.

TEACHING CONCEPTS

With your students, read, briefly explain and demonstrate the concepts as they are introduced.

- **Steady Beat**
- **Quarter note** ♩

   Speaking Rhythms System: say "ta"

   Clapping Rhythms System: one clap
- **Quarter rest** 𝄽

   Speaking Rhythms System: say "sh"

   Clapping Rhythms System: one shake (a gesture with both hands which resembles shaking water from one's hands)

   Choose either a speaking or clapping counting system for your students and stick with it.
- **Barline and Measure**
- **Repeat Sign**

TEACHING SEQUENCE FOR EXERCISES

1. Teacher establishes a slow, steady beat.
2. Students play the beat so that it is kinesthetically felt. Using the speaking rhythms system, students play the beat by lightly patting a hand on their lap. Using the clapping rhythms system, students play the beat by lightly tapping their foot.
3. Teacher provides preparatory count-off, "ONE two ready begin" and then students speak or clap the rhythm of the exercise while at the same time playing the steady beat.
4. Once perfected *a cappella,* then students perform the exercise with the play-along CD accompaniment. CD Track 8 is a four-measure accompaniment and CD Track 9 is an eight-measure accompaniment. Use the appropriate track as indicated at the beginning of the exercise.

Begin With the Beat

Keep It Steady

Just as our hearts beat with an even pulse, the beat is the steady pulse which underlies all music.

Quarter Note and Quarter Rest

♩ = Quarter Note = One beat of sound   ♪ = Quarter Rest = One beat of silence

Ex. 1

Barline and Measure

Barlines (|) are used to group music notes and rests together.
The area between two barlines is called a *measure*.

Barline   Measure   Barline

Any number of beats may be grouped in a measure. There are four beats per measure in the exercises below.

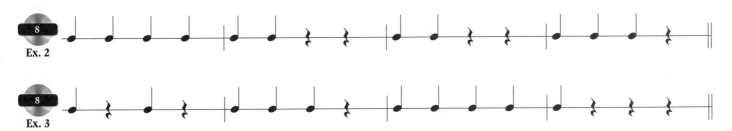

Ex. 2

Ex. 3

Repeat

The repeat sign (:‖) is used to indicate that a section of music should be repeated.

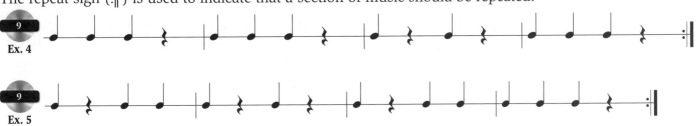

Ex. 4

Ex. 5

Add DO and RE

MORE KEYS TO SIGHT-SINGING SUCCESS

- Require each student to play the beat.
- Develop independence from the beginning. Encourage students to sight-sing the exercises on their own as a group, *a cappella*. Avoid the temptation to sight-sing out loud with the students.
- Encourage students to keep going when a mistake is made. Don't stop. Encourage them to keep their eyes moving forward with the tempo so they may resume sight-singing until the end of the exercise.
- Introduce concepts well, but be quick and succinct. Keep students involved in *making* music as opposed to discussing music.
- Steady progress is the goal. Don't try to accomplish too much, too fast. Sight-singing is a challenging activity. Consistent daily practice, even for just a few minutes, is the key to success!

TEACHING CONCEPTS

With your students, read, briefly explain and demonstrate aurally the concepts as they are introduced.

- **Pitch**
- **Staff:** Explain that although the music staff is like a ladder, notes appear up and down on *both lines* and *spaces*.
- **Introduce *Do* and *Re*:** Make sure students recognize the difference between *Do* and *Re* both visually and aurally.

Option: If students ask, introduce treble clef.

TEACHING SEQUENCE FOR EXERCISES

First begin with the rhythm alone:

1. Teacher establishes a slow, steady beat.
2. Students play the beat so that it is kinesthetically felt.
3. Teacher provides preparatory count-off, "ONE two ready begin" and then students speak or clap the rhythm of the exercise while at the same time playing the steady beat.

> *Then do the exercise again adding pitch:*
> 1. Teacher establishes *Do* (C) aurally.
> 2. Teacher provides preparatory count-off, "ONE two ready begin" and then students sight-sing the pitches (ex. *do do re re*) in rhythm while at the same time playing the steady beat.

Once perfected *a cappella*, then students perform the exercise with the play-along CD accompaniment. Use Tracks 10 or 11 as indicated at the beginning of the exercise.

Add DO and RE

Adding Pitch to the Beat

Pitch is how high or low each note sounds. A music note is placed on the staff to indicate its pitch. The staff is like a ladder. Notes placed near the bottom of the staff sound lower than notes placed higher on the staff.

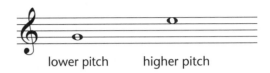

lower pitch   higher pitch

Introducing *Do*

Do is often the pitch which represents the home base, sometimes called the home tone or keynote. *Do* can be assigned to any pitch, but for now we will assign it to the pitch, C.

Meet Re

Re is the upper next-door neighbor note to *Do*. If *Do* is the note C, then *Re* is the note D.

Introduce Meter and MI

MORE KEYS TO SIGHT-SINGING SUCCESS

- Allow a student to set the tempo and/or conduct the group through an exercise.
- Be alert to student successes and praise them sincerely when they do well. Most younger children enjoy being praised individually. Older students often do not wish to be singled out among their peers, but they do however, enjoy praise which is directed to the whole group.
- Create a classroom climate where mistakes are treated as challenges rather than problems.
- Refrain from singing with the students. Get them started and then let them proceed alone.
- Promote confidence and success. Encourage students to **concentrate, Concentrate, CONCENTRATE** and make every attempt to sight-sing the exercise correctly the first time.
- Commit at least 3 to 5 minutes for sight-singing during each rehearsal or class period and be consistent.
- Make use of the teachable moment. If students ask questions, provide more in-depth explanations.

TEACHING CONCEPTS

With your students, read, briefly explain and demonstrate the concepts as they are introduced.

- **$\frac{4}{4}$ Meter**: At this time it is not necessary to go into great detail while explaining this concept. Students do need to understand the concept that in $\frac{4}{4}$ time there will be four beats per measure.
- **Introducing Mi**: Make sure that students recognize the difference between *Do*, *Re* and *Mi* both visually and aurally.
- **Half note:** ♩
  Speaking system: say "ta-ah"
  Clapping system: clap-squeeze
  Half rest: ▬
  say "sh-sh"
  two "shakes"

TEACHING SEQUENCE FOR EXERCISES

First begin with the rhythm alone:

1. Teacher establishes a slow, steady beat.
2. Students play the beat so that it is kinesthetically felt.
3. Teacher provides preparatory count-off, "ONE two ready begin" and then students speak or clap the rhythm of the exercise while at the same time playing the steady beat.

Then do the exercise again adding pitch:

1. Teacher establishes *Do* (C) aurally. *
2. Teacher provides preparatory count-off, "ONE two ready begin" and then students sight-sing the pitches (ex. *do do re mi*) in rhythm while at the same time playing the steady beat.

Once perfected *a cappella*, then students perform the exercise with the play-along CD accompaniment. Use Tracks 12 or 13 as indicated at the beginning of the exercise.

* Note that exercises 4 and 5 on page 15 begin on the syllable *Mi*. Just prior to performing this exercise using pitches, point this out to the students. Explain that you will give them the pitch for *Do*, the home base and then they will need to sing in their heads the pitch sequence: *do-re-mi* to find the starting pitch. In the beginning, demonstrate this aurally for the students. The eventual goal however is to have them find the starting pitch on their own.

Introduce Meter and MI

Time Signature: $\frac{4}{4}$ Meter

A *time signature* (sometimes called a *meter signature*) is a set of numbers which appear at the beginning of a piece of music.

4 The top number shows the number of beats per measure.

4 The bottom number shows the kind of note that represents the beat (4 means quarter note).

Sing: Do   Re

Introducing Mi

Mi is the upper next-door neighbor note to *Re*. If *Do* is the note C and *Re* is the note D, then *Mi* is the note E.

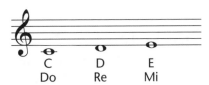

C   D   E
Do   Re   Mi

Sing: Do   Mi

Half Note and Half Rest

Half Note   *Half Rest*

A *half note* represents two beats of sound when the quarter note represents the beat.
A *half rest* represents two beats of silence when the quarter note represents the beat.

Sing: Do

Ex. 4
Sing: Mi

Ex. 5
Sing: Mi

Add Neighbors FA and SOL

MORE KEYS TO SIGHT-SINGING SUCCESS

- Continue to maintain consistent practice. Steady progress is the goal!
- Challenge students by increasing the tempo of the exercise.
- Be sure to introduce concepts well, but be quick and succinct. Keep students *making* music, rather than talking about music.
- Develop a helpful classroom atmosphere where mistakes are treated as challenges rather than problems. Allow no student to make fun of another person's honest mistake.
- Although entirely optional, the Accompaniment CD is a highly motivational tool for success.
- Challenge: Divide the class into two groups. Assign a different exercise to each group and have them sight-read these parts simultaneously. Choose exercises with the same CD numbers for harmonious part-singing.

TEACHING CONCEPTS

With your students, read, briefly explain and demonstrate the concepts as they are introduced.

- **Adding *Fa* and *Sol*:** Make sure that students recognize the difference between *Do, Re, Mi, Fa* and *Sol* both visually and aurally.

- **Dotted Half Note:**
  Speaking system: say "ta-ah-ah"
  Clapping system: clap-squeeze-squeeze

- **Whole Note:**
  Speaking system: say "ta-ah-ah-ah"
  Clapping system: clap-squeeze-squeeze-squeeze

- **Whole Rest:**
  Speaking system: say "sh-sh-sh-sh"
  Clapping system: four shakes

TEACHING SEQUENCE FOR EXERCISES

First begin with the rhythm alone:

1. Teacher establishes a slow, steady beat.
2. Students play the beat so that it is kinesthetically felt.
3. Teacher provides preparatory count-off, "ONE two ready begin" and then students speak or clap the rhythm of the exercise while at the same time playing the steady beat.

> *Then do the exercise again adding pitch:*
> 1. Teacher establishes *Do* (C) aurally.*
> 2. Teacher provides preparatory count-off, "ONE two ready begin" and then students sight-sing the pitches (ex. *do do re mi*) in rhythm while at the same time playing the steady beat.

Once perfected *a cappella*, then students perform the exercise with the play-along CD accompaniment. Use Tracks 14 or 15 as indicated at the beginning of the exercise.

* Note that exercises 4 and 5 (pg. 17) begin on the syllables *Mi* and *Sol* respectively. Explain that you will give them the pitch for *Do*, the home base and then they will need to sing in their heads the pitch sequence: *do-re-mi-fa-sol* to find the starting pitch. In the beginning, demonstrate this aurally for the students. However, the eventual goal is to have them find the starting pitch on their own.

Add Neighbors FA and SOL

Adding More Upper Neighbors

Fa is the upper next-door neighbor note to *Mi*, and *Sol* is the upper next-door neighbor to *Fa*. If *Do* is the note C, then *Fa* is the note F and *Sol* is the note G.

C   D   E   F   G
Do   Re   Mi   Fa   Sol

14
Ex. 1

Sing: Do   Fa   Sol

14
Ex. 2

Sing: Do

Dotted Half Note

Dotted Half Note

Whole Note and Whole Rest

Whole Note   *Whole Rest*

A *dotted half note* represents three beats of sound when the quarter note represents the beat.

A *whole note* represents four beats of sound when the quarter note represents the beat.

A *whole rest* represents four beats of silence when the quarter note represents the beat.

14
Ex. 3
Sing: Do

15
Ex. 4
Sing: Mi

15
Ex. 5
Sing: Sol

Neighbor LA Joins In

MORE KEYS TO SIGHT-SINGING SUCCESS

- Maintain a positive classroom environment. *Be enthusiastic!*
- Periodically review and practice previously learned exercises.
- Move among the students as they sight-sing to assess and help individuals.
- Challenge: Divide the class into two groups. Assign a different exercise to each group and have them sight-read these parts simultaneously. Choose exercises with the same CD numbers for harmonious part-singing.
- After a rhythm exercise is learned well, students often enjoy repeating the exercise again using an unpitched mouth sound such as "ch" or "ts."
- Accompany the students *ad lib.* on an instrument of your choice.

TEACHING CONCEPTS

With your students, read, briefly explain and demonstrate the concepts as they are introduced.

- **Eighth Notes:** Make sure that students understand that eighth notes move twice as fast as quarter notes.
  Speaking system: say "ti-ti"
  Clapping system: clap-clap
- **Adding *La*:** Make sure that students recognize the syllable *La*, both visually and auarally.

TEACHING SEQUENCE FOR EXERCISES

First begin with the rhythm alone:

1. Teacher establishes a slow, steady beat.
2. Students play the beat so that it is kinesthetically felt.
3. Teacher provides preparatory count-off, "ONE two ready begin" and then students speak or clap the rhythm of the exercise while at the same time playing the steady beat.

Then do the exercise again adding pitch:

1. Teacher establishes *Do* (C) aurally.*
2. Teacher provides preparatory count-off, "ONE two ready begin" and then students sight-sing the pitches (ex. *do do re mi*) in rhythm while at the same time playing the steady beat.

Once perfected *a cappella*, then students perform the exercise with the play-along CD accompaniment. Use Tracks 16, 17 or 18 as indicated at the beginning of the exercise.

*Note that exercise 6 (pg. 19) begins on the syllable *Mi*, and exercise 7 begins on the syllable *Sol*. Explain that you will give them the pitch for *Do*, the home base and then they will need to sing in their heads the pitch sequence: *do-re-mi-fa-sol* to find the starting pitch. In the beginning, demonstrate this aurally for the students. The eventual goal however is to have the students find the starting pitch on their own.

Neighbor LA Joins In

Quicker Rhythm – Eighth Notes

Two Eighth Notes (♫) = One beat of sound

An eighth note is a note that represents half a beat of sound when the quarter note represents the beat. Two eighth notes together equal one beat of sound when the quarter note represents the beat.

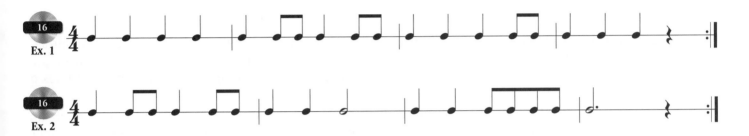

Adding Another Upper Neighbor: *La*

La is the upper next-door neighbor note to *Sol*.
If *Do* is the note C, then *La* is the note A.

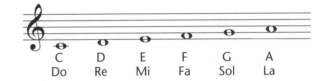

Sing: Do   La

Sing: Do

Sing: Do

Sing: Mi

Sing: Sol

Finish Off With TI and DO

MORE KEYS TO SIGHT-SINGING SUCCESS

- Encourage students to imagine mentally how an exercise will sound prior to sight-singing it.
- Choose a student to accompany the group *ad lib.* on a percussion instrument or other instrument of choice.

TEACHING CONCEPTS

- With your students, read, briefly explain and demonstrate the concepts as they are introduced.
- **Adding *Ti* and High *Do*:** Make sure that students recognize *Ti* and high *Do* both visually and aurally. Let them hear *Do* and high *Do* simultaneously, so they can hear the octave. Explain that when sight-singing, high *Do* is simply sung "*Do.*" Optional: Explain and demonstrate the concept that the *pattern* continues on above high *Do* and extends downward below *Do*.
- **Skips:** It is important to solidly establish these skips aurally in the students' minds prior to sight-singing the exercises. In preparation for the exercises, using the syllables, demonstrate skips between these pitches aurally in a variety of configurations. Then do various echo patterns with the students using these pitches.

TEACHING SEQUENCE FOR EXERCISES

First begin with the rhythm alone:

1. Teacher establishes a slow, steady beat.
2. Students play the beat so that it is kinesthetically felt.
3. Teacher provides preparatory count-off, "ONE two ready begin" and then students speak or clap the rhythm of the exercise while at the same time playing the steady beat.

Then do the exercise again adding pitch:

1. Teacher establishes *Do* (C) aurally.*
2. Teacher provides preparatory count-off, "ONE two ready begin" and then students sight-sing the pitches in rhythm while at the same time playing the steady beat.

Once perfected *a cappella*, then students perform the exercise with the play-along CD accompaniment. Use Tracks 19, 20 or 21 as indicated at the beginning of the exercise.

*Note that exercises 2 and 3 (pg. 20) begin on the syllables high *Do* and *Sol*, respectively, and exercises 5 and 6 begin on *Sol* and high *Do*. Explain that you will give them the pitch for *Do*, the home base and then they will need to sing in their heads the pitch sequence: *do-re-mi-fa-sol-la-ti-do* to find the starting pitch. In the beginning, demonstrate this aurally for the students. The eventual goal however is to have the students find the starting pitch on their own.

Sing a Song!

On pages 22-23, there is a new song that incorporates the sight-singing skills which have been learned after completing these lessons. Introduce the two staves, pointing out that they will be learning the music in the top staff only at first. Follow the same sight-singing sequence as has been used for the previous exercises. You may wish to divide the piece into segments (such as 12 measures) and have students completely learn one segment before moving on to the next. Once perfected *a cappella*, then increase the tempo. Then have the students perform the song with the CD accompaniment on track 23. (NOTE: a full performance version of the song can be found on track 22.)

Finish Off With TI and DO

Adding More Upper Neighbors: *Ti* and High *Do*

Ti is the upper next-door neighbor note to *La*, and *High Do*
is the upper next-door neighbor note to *Ti*. If *Do* is the note C,
then *Ti* is the note B and *High Do* is the note C.

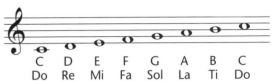

Skips

As you know, notes step up and down on the lines
and spaces of the staff, which is like a ladder. In
doing so, melodies are created. Sometimes music
notes move in skips rather than steps.

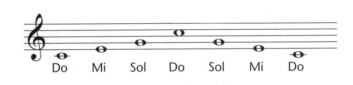

Piano PDF on Enhanced CD

22 — Full Performance
23 — Accompaniment

(2 measures introduction)

Sing a Song!

**Words and Music by
AUDREY SNYDER**

Part I (mel.)

(Mi)
Sing, sing, sing a song. Sing, sing, sing a song. Sing a

Part II (opt.)

(Mi)
Sing, sing, sing a song. Sing, sing, sing a song.

song of joy, sing a song of hope.

Come cel-e-brate the spir-it. Let ev-'ry-bod-y hear it.

Ev-'ry-bod-y sing, ev-'ry-bod-y sing, sing a song.

Ev-'ry-bod-y sing, ev-'ry-bod-y sing, sing a song.

When we get to feel-ing sor-ry for our-selves, when we get to feel-ing

Oo

down, if we can just re-mem-ber all the good things that we have;

If we can just re-mem-ber all the good things that we have;

May I Have a Drumroll, Please? It's the Drumline!

by Brad Shank

People all over the world enjoy playing drums and other percussion instruments. Maybe even you do, too! In many countries there are special groups of drums and drummers. These drumming groups play at parties, festivals, holidays, and other special times.

In the United States, there are many different kinds of drumming groups. One kind of drumming group that is special in the United States is found in a marching band. If you have ever seen a marching band perform, then you have heard these special drummers. They are called the drumline.

Drumlines

There are usually four instruments in a drumline: cymbals, snare drums, tenor drums, and bass drums. Drumlines do many things for the marching band. They play their percussion sounds along with melody instruments like trumpets, flutes, and tubas. They also help the band march in step exactly together.

Drums have been played in marching bands for hundreds of years. Marching bands started in the military. The drums in the marching band helped soldiers march together. Sometimes the drums even played special rhythms to send secret instructions to the soldiers!

Cadence Crazy!

Sometimes, the drumline does something very special—they play a cadence. A cadence is an exciting time when the drumline plays all by itself. When the cadence starts, you hear the pops of the tenor drum, the sizzle of the snare, the crash of the cymbals, and the booming bass drum. The drummers whip their sticks and mallets up and down. They keep your ears and your eyes busy!

Ready, March!

Play each rhythm pattern at the top of page 25. Then try to play them together. All the instruments together make a drumline!

Introducing…the Drumline

The **bass drum** is the biggest drum. It hangs from the shoulders in front of the musician. The drummer hits the side of the drum with a large mallet. This makes a very low, loud sound that goes "Boom!"

The **snare drum** makes a fast "rat-a-tat-tat" sound. Snare drummers have some strange names for the rhythms they play, like the paradiddle and the flam.

When you see a band, you can't miss the **tenor drums**. Three or four tenor drums hang flat in front of one drummer. Each drum has a different pitch.

Cymbals are exciting to play because they make a huge "CRASH!" They are very important to the other drummers. The other drummers listen for the cymbals so they all play together at the same tempo.

Basic Drumline Rhythms

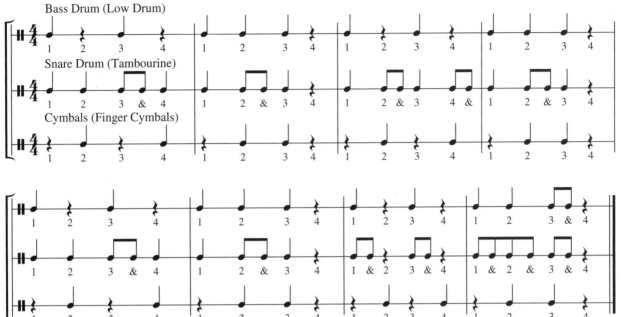

Yankee Doodle

Traditional
Arranged by JOHN HIGGINS

(4-measure introduction)

5 Verse

1. Yan - kee Doo - dle went to town a - rid - ing on a po - ny. He
2. Fath'r and I went down to camp a - long with Cap - tain Good - in'. And

stuck a feath - er in his cap and called it mac - a - ro - ni. }
there we saw the men and boys as thick as has - ty pud - din'. }

9 Refrain

Yan - kee Doo - dle keep it up, Yan - kee Doo - dle dand - y.

8

Mind the mu - sic and the step, and with the girls be hand - y.

Rock and Roll Rhythms

Suggested Instruments

Part 1: Tambourine   **Part 2: Shakers**   **Part 3: Rhythm Sticks**   **Part 4: Bass Drum**

Body Percussion

As a first step in learning the unpitched percussion parts on the next page, have the students use the following body percussion.

Part 1: hand claps accenting beats 2 and 4 (the "back beats")

Part 2: palm swishes (rubbing palms back and forth to create a "swishing" sound) for the even eighth note rhythm

Part 3: finger snaps

Part 4: chest "thump" with an open palm

Percussion Instruments

1. Once the students can perform the unpitched parts on body percussion, distribute instruments to be played on Part 1 (tambourine), Part 2 (shakers), Part 3 (rhythm sticks or actual drumsticks) and Part 4 (bass drum).

2. Use the instruction track (CD track 27) to learn how to play the four rhythms. Students not playing instruments may play the rhythms using body percussion. Rotate the students playing the instruments. Every student should get a chance to play at least one rhythm using an instrument.

3. Use the play-along track (CD track 28) when the students can play the rhythms confidently.

Pitched Instruments

The pitched instruments are **optional**. Any pitched instruments may be used, but instrument suggestions and parts are provided. Eventually, combine these pitched parts with the un-pitched instrument parts.

The piano part (below) is optional as well. It can be added at your discretion. These parts match the harmony played on the play-along track and may be taught by rote.

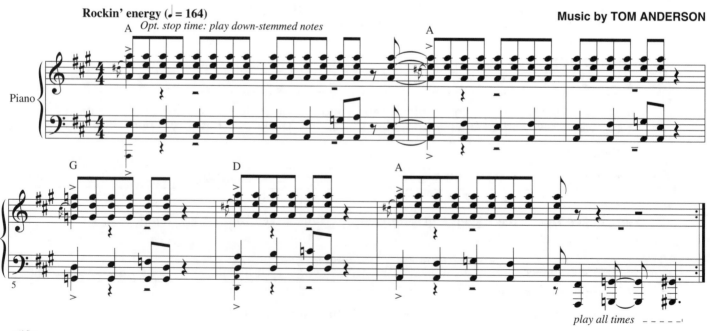

Rockin' energy (♩ = 164)

Music by TOM ANDERSON

Opt. stop time: play down-stemmed notes

play all times

Give me that rock and roll music! People have been saying that since the 1950s — and continue to say it all over the world. With its driving rhythm and steady eighth notes, it captured the hearts (and feet!) of teenagers craving a new kind of music.

Accent the second and fourth beats – the *back beats* – if you are playing Part 1. Play even eighth notes with Part 2. Click those sticks with authority in Part 3. And give the drummers some syncopation on the low end in Part 4.

Unpitched

Rockin' Energy! ($\quad$ = 164)

Music by TOM ANDERSON

Pitched

Opt. stop time: play down-stemmed notes

Classroom Instrument

29 Full Performance **30** Accompaniment

C. C. Rider
(pitched instruments)

Traditional
Arranged by TOM ANDERSON

Notes Used: C, D, E, F, G, A, B, C'

Blues Shuffle (♩ = 112)

5 17 29* D.S.

Play 4 times

mf

(4th time)
To Coda ⊕

⊕ **CODA**

* Pitched instruments

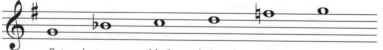

Set up instruments with these pitches. Improvise a solo
with these notes the 3rd time through the song (meas. 29).

C. C. Rider
(vocals)

Traditional
Arranged by TOM ANDERSON

Copyright © 2005 by HAL LEONARD CORPORATION
International Copyright Secured All Rights Reserved

Follow the Drinkin' Gourd

African-American Spiritual
Arranged by CRISTI CARY MILLER and KATHLYN REYNOLDS

(4-measure introduction, perform entire song twice)

Refrain

Teaching Suggestions

1. To introduce this song, take time to discuss its story and historical background. (A spiritual with instructions embedded in the words to follow the drinking gourd or "Big Dipper." The handle of this constellation points to the North Star that helped guide the slaves to freedom.)

2. Use a copy of the song to give your students. Sing the melody on "loo" as students follow the melodic line. Stop randomly and ask them to identify the word on which you stopped. Repeat process several times. Add the words and sing until secure.

Orff Teaching Suggestions

1. Alternately pat the BX pattern using a crossover motion while speaking the "think" words. They will play this pattern for the entire song except during the verse. Transfer to instrument.

2. Play the AX/SX pattern in the air using "think" words and moving hands to show pitch changes. Transfer to instruments. Play against the BX part while singing.

3. Alternately snap the AG/SG ostinato while speaking "think" words. Transfer to instruments.

4. Add the metallophone part to the verse measures and include in ensemble.

5. Clap the hand drum ostinato while speaking the "think" words. Transfer to instrument(s).

6. Sing and play together.

Full Performance

Play-Along with a Rock Band

By Tom Anderson
Lesson Plan by Janet Day

Recorder Play-Along with a ROCK BAND

Recording has 4 clicks, then 8 measures introduction

Play 3 times

B   A   G

Copyright © 2010 by HAL LEONARD CORPORATION
International Copyright Secured All Rights Reserved

TEACHING SUGGESTIONS

1. Distribute instruments and a visual of each part via projection or reproduced part for each player (PDFs on Enhanced CD). You may choose to use ALL parts, or just a few depending on level of players.

2. Before you begin, explain or review the following:
   - Note & Rest values
   - Dynamics: *mf, f*
   - Repeat Signs
   - 1st/2nd/3rd Endings
   - Multi-measure rest
   - Accents
   - Recorder fingerings (B, A, G)

3. Option 1: Teach each part individually using your preferred method.

4. Option 2: Beginning at a slow tempo, challenge students to read their music skillfully the first time through. Increase the tempo as students are comfortable.

5. When all parts are secure, play along with the full performance recording (CD track 33).

Mallets Play-Along with a ROCK BAND

Recording has 4 clicks, then 8 measures introduction

Play 3 times

Alto Xylophone

Bass Xylophone

Recording has 4 clicks, then 8 measures introduction

Play 3 times

Alto Metallophone

Recording has 4 clicks, then 8 measures introduction

Play 3 times

34 Full Performance

 35 Accompaniment

Ragtime B-A-G

THE ENTERTAINER
By Scott Joplin
Arranged by Janet Day

Recording has 4 clicks, then begin

Ragtime (♩ = 100-120)

Need to Know

- Recorder fingerings for B, A, G
- 4/4 time signature

- ♩. ♩ ♩ ♫ ‌‌𝄾
- tie
- **f** (forte)

- **mf** (mezzo forte)
- repeat sign
- 1st and 2nd endings

TIP: Play measure 7 without the tie (as two eighth notes), then add the tie by holding through the second note.

Ragtime B-A-G

Recording has 4 clicks, then begin

THE ENTERTAINER
By Scott Joplin
Arranged by Janet Day

Ragtime B-A-G

Recording has 4 clicks, then begin

THE ENTERTAINER
By Scott Joplin
Arranged by Janet Day

Makin' Music All Day Long

Partner I

Words and Music by
JOHN JACOBSON and MAC HUFF
Arranged by MAC HUFF

(8 measures introduction)

Hey! We're mak-in' mu-sic, see, we're mak-in' mu-sic, it's a hap-py day. If you got the no-tion, get your-self in mo-tion, sing it your own way. Do your-self a fa-vor, bring a-long a neigh-bor, sing your fav-'rite song. We're mak-in' mu-sic all day long! We're mak-in' mu-sic all day, we're mak-in' mu-sic all day long! Mu-sic all day long!

Making music with friends can be fun.
Learn these two melodies and then sing them together.
What instrument will you play?

Partner II

(8 measures introduction)

9 *Sing 2nd and 3rd times*
Part II

Wah - wah! Can you hear the trum-pet? Oom - pah - pah! A lit - tle

tu - ba too. Rat - at - tat - tat! Noth-ing like a drum-mer.

17 Blue - hoo. A clar - i - net will do. La - la. I

feel so hap-py. La - la. We can't go wrong.

Clap We're mak - in' mu - sic all day long!

1, 2

3 *Clap* We're mak - in' mu - sic all day,

Clap we're mak - in' mu - sic all day long!

Mu - sic all day long!

Piano
PDF on
Enhanced
CD

38 Full Performance **39** Accompaniment

She'll Be Comin' 'Round the Mountain

(Partner I)

Traditional Folksong
Arranged by MARY DONNELLY and GEORGE L.O. STRID

Hoedown feel (♩ = 90)
(Sing 1st and 3rd times)

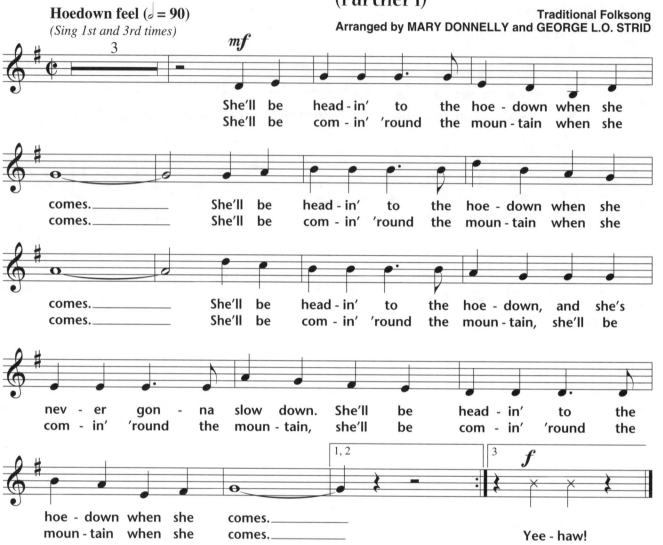

She'll be head-in' to the hoe-down when she
She'll be com-in' 'round the moun-tain when she

comes._____ She'll be head-in' to the hoe-down when she
comes._____ She'll be com-in' 'round the moun-tain when she

comes._____ She'll be head-in' to the hoe-down, and she's
comes._____ She'll be com-in' 'round the moun-tain, she'll be

nev-er gon-na slow down. She'll be head-in' to the
com-in' 'round the moun-tain, she'll be com-in' 'round the

hoe-down when she comes._____
moun-tain when she comes._____

1, 2 | **3** ***f***

Yee-haw!

The original purchaser of this book has permission to reproduce this songsheet for educational use in one school only. Any other use is strictly prohibited.

Movement Idea

- Formation: students stand in a circle and number off by twos. All hold hands.
- Phrase 1: all circle eight steps to the left.
- Phrase 2: circle eight steps to the right.
- Phrase 3: ones and twos hook right elbows and walk in a circle.
- Phrase 4: hook left elbows and walk in a circle.
- During the interlude, ones stay where they are and twos move one person to the left to a new partner. Repeat for all three verses. Have students wear bandanas, cowboy hats, western shirts, long skirts/dresses and perform for another class.

She'll Be Headin' to a Hoedown

(Partner II)

Hoedown feel (♩ = 90)
(Sing 2nd and 3rd times)

Words and Music by MARY DONNELLY and GEORGE L.O. STRID

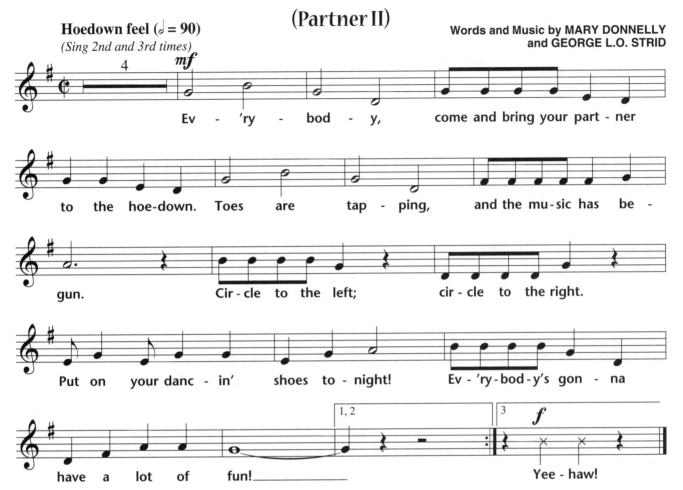

Ev - 'ry - bod - y, come and bring your part - ner to the hoe-down. Toes are tap - ping, and the mu - sic has be - gun. Cir - cle to the left; cir - cle to the right. Put on your danc - in' shoes to - night! Ev - 'ry-bod-y's gon - na have a lot of fun!_____ Yee - haw!

OK TO REPRODUCE

Movement Idea

- Formation: Square Dance set of four couples
- Introduction: Honor your partners; honor your corners.
- Phrase 1: all join hands and circle left.
- Phrase 2: circle right.
- Phrase 3: do-si-do your partners.
- Phrase 4: swing your partners.
- Repeat for each verse.

If your students balk at holding hands, perhaps you could do a simple line dance such as:
- Phrase 1: starting with left foot, take eight steps in a circle to the left and clap on beat 8.
- Phrase 2: same as phrase one, starting on the right foot and circling to the right.
- Phrase 3: starting on left foot, side step to the left, together, step, touch. Repeat to the right.
- Phrase 4: starting on left foot, step forward L, R, L touch, then backwards R, L, R and turn one-quarter turn to the right.
- Repeat for each verse. This is very basic. Feel free to add your own steps.

This Little Light of Mine

African-American Spiritual
Arranged by EMILY CROCKER

4 measures introduction

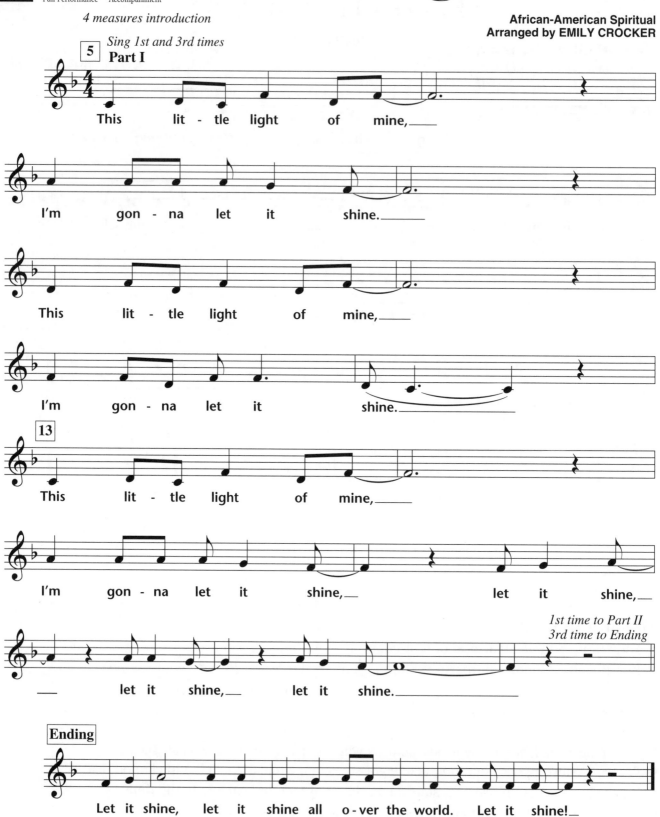

5 *Sing 1st and 3rd times*
Part I

This lit - tle light of mine,____

I'm gon - na let it shine.____

This lit - tle light of mine,____

I'm gon - na let it shine.____

13

This lit - tle light of mine,____

I'm gon - na let it shine,__ let it shine,__

1st time to Part II
3rd time to Ending

__ let it shine,__ let it shine.____

Ending

Let it shine, let it shine all o - ver the world. Let it shine!__

Most African Americans are descendents of the slaves who were brought to this country even before it was an independent nation. To keep their spirits up through their terrible ordeals, they sang songs. They sang songs of hope. They sang songs of sadness. Out of the darkness of their lives, they sang songs of light!

Piano
PDF on
Enhanced
CD

42
Full Performance

43
Accompaniment

Zum Gali Gali
(Partner I)

Traditional Folksong
Arranged by MARY DONNELLY
and GEORGE L.O. STRID

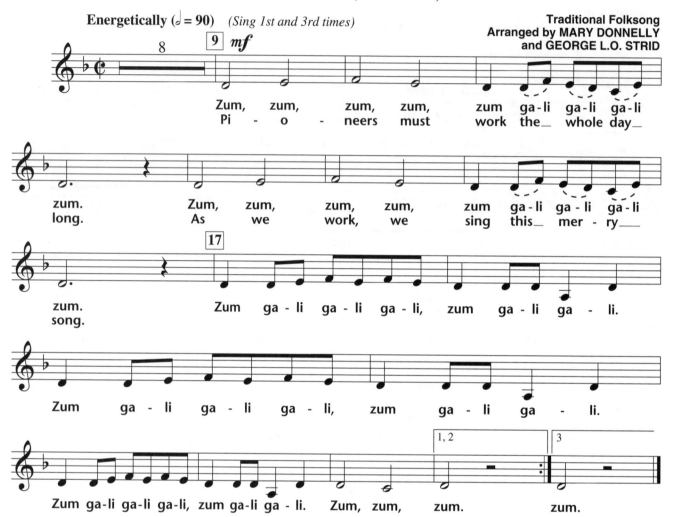

OK TO
REPRODUCE

MOVEMENT IDEA

Do a simplified hora-style dance.

Suggested steps:

1. Have students stand in a circle, arms linked or holding hands. There will be two steps per measure.

2. On phrase one (measures 9-10), step in towards the center four steps raising hands gradually

3. On phrase two (measures 11-12), step out four steps and lower hands.

4. Repeat for phrases three and four (measures 13-16).

5. At measure 17, circle to the left stepping on the strong beats.

6. Option for upper grades: At measure 17, do a grapevine to the left for five steps. On beat six, kick right foot. On beat seven, put right foot down. On beat eight, kick left foot. Repeat as necessary.

The Pioneer's Song
(Partner II)

Energetically (♩ = 90)

(Sing 2nd and 3rd times)

Words and Music by MARY DONNELLY
and GEORGE L.O. STRID

We sing as we work to-geth-er
The pi-o-neers work the land, to-

in the noon-day sun. We join our hands to-geth-er
geth-er hand in hand. We work the whole day long, and

till the work is done! } Sing, lai* lai lai, lai-di
raise our voic-es in song.

lai lai, lai-di lai-di lai. Sing, lai lai lai, lai-di

lai lai lai lai lai. lai.

1, 2 *3*

* "lai" pronounced *lye*; "di" pronounced *dee*

OSTINATO ACTIVITY

1. Have one group of students learn the following ostinato on a barred classroom instrument.

2. Teach this ostinato to a different group of students.

3. Have students play both ostinatos with these partner songs.

Active Listening Lessons

By Wesley Ball

Article Worksheet
Aaron Copland

Name _____ Class _____

ABOUT THE COMPOSER

Aaron Copland (1900-1990) was born in Brooklyn, NY—the youngest of five children. His older sister gave him piano lessons. He quickly advanced and became interested in composing his own music. After studying with a local teacher, Aaron left home at age 20, traveling to Paris to study with the famous teacher of composition, Nadia Boulanger. She encouraged young Copland to incorporate American "elements" in his music.

He wrote *John Henry*—a piece for orchestra that tells the story of the American folk hero who competed with the "iron horse" (steam locomotive). Copland also wrote music for three ballets: *Billy the Kid*, *Rodeo*, and *Appalachian Spring*. From 1939-1949, he wrote music for seven movies. And he even wrote an opera for high school students, *The Second Hurricane*.

Aaron Copland was one of America's greatest composers.

Answer each question in the space provided.

1. What year was Aaron Copland born? _____

2. Where was he born? _____

3. When Copland was a child, he took lessons from whom? _____

4. At age 20, he left home to study composition with _____.

5. An "iron horse" is the nickname for a _____ _____.

6. Copland wrote music for movies. He even wrote an opera for high school students. Its title is

   _____ _____ _____.

Follow the instruments on this chart as you listen to the music. Play hand drums where they are indicated (3rd row). You will hear timpani in the music.

Fanfare for the Common Man
by Aaron Copland

START

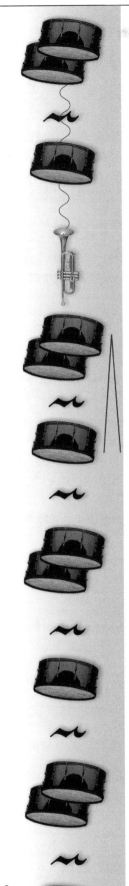
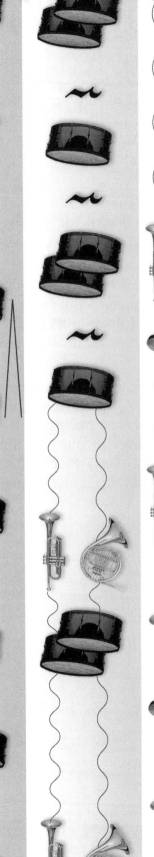
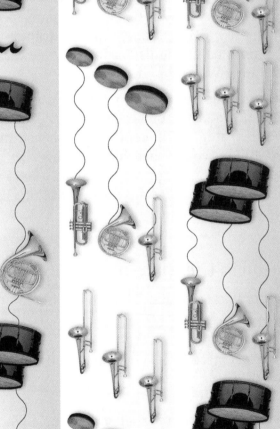
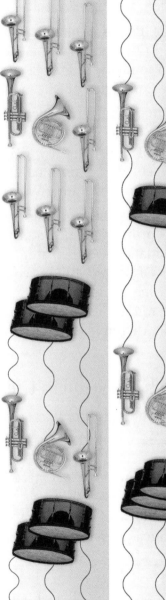

END

Article Worksheet
Benjamin Britten

Name _____ Class _____

People should not have been surprised when 6 year-old Benjamin Britten began composing music. After all, he was born on November 22 – St. Cecilia's Day – a day that honors Saint Cecilia, the patron saint of music! Growing up in Suffolk, England, he had a brother and two sisters. His father was a dentist and amateur singer. Young Benjamin first studied piano, then viola. At age 17, he entered the Royal College of Music in London, winning several prizes for his compositions.

Throughout his life, he admired the music of many musicians, but none more than that of Henry Purcell. Like his hero, Britten also wrote a "Hymn to St. Cecilia." Purcell had written the first English opera, and Britten wanted to follow in Purcell's footsteps. Throughout his lifetime, he wrote 14 operas. *Gloriana* was written for the Coronation of Queen Elizabeth II.

Britten was a man with strong beliefs. He felt that war was no way for people to settle their differences. It bothered him greatly when World War II killed so many people and destroyed so many beautiful buildings. In 1961, he composed a *War Requiem*, paying tribute to all people who had lost their lives in war. The *Requiem* was performed at the dedication of a new cathedral, replacing Coventry Cathedral, which had been bombed during World War II.

In 1946, the British government asked Britten to write a piece of music for a movie that would introduce young people to the instruments of the orchestra. Britten decided to compose a *Theme and Variations*, where each variation would feature a different family of instruments. But first, he needed a theme—a main melody! Of course, Britten could have made up his own melody, but he decided to go back in history, borrowing a theme from his fellow countryman, Henry Purcell. The *theme* for Britten's *Young Person's Guide to the Orchestra* is taken from a rondo that Purcell had written for background music in a play. It's a bold, rhythmic theme in D minor.

Answer each question in the space provided.

1. Benjamin Britten was born on November 22 – a day that many musicians celebrate, paying tribute to whom? _____

2. Like Purcell, Britten wrote a piece of music to honor the Queen of England – Queen Elizabeth II. What was the name of the opera? _____

3. Britten wrote a piece of music in honor of all of the people who had been killed in war? The title of the piece was _____.

4. Britten composed the piece about the war in what year? _____

5. Purcell's theme is used in Britten's _____ _____ _____ to the _____ which introduced the instruments of the orchestra.

The Young Person's Guide to the Orchestra

THEME by Benjamin Britten

Listen to the *theme* played by full orchestra, the woodwinds, brass, strings, percussion, and full orchestra. When is the music loud? How loud is it? When does the music get softer? When does it get louder?

Review these dynamic markings:

	p	*mp*	*mf*	*f*	*ff*	*fff*
Italian:	piano	mezzo-piano	mezzo-forte	forte	fortissimo	fortississimo
English:	soft	medium soft	medium loud	loud	very loud	very, very loud

crescendo

getting louder

decrescendo

getting softer

Listen to the music and write the dynamic markings below the pictures.

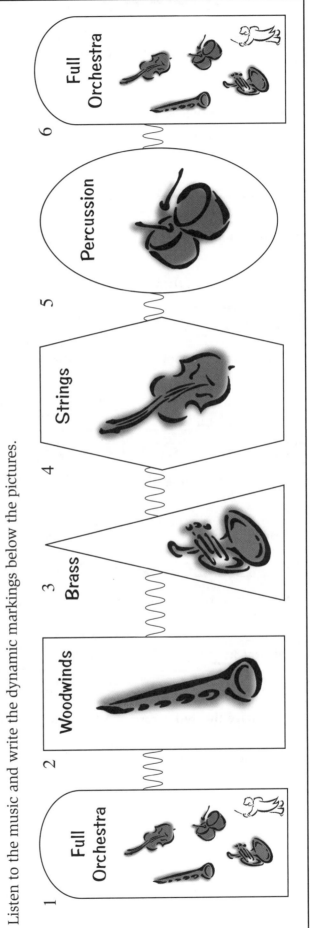

1 Full Orchestra

2 Woodwinds

3 Brass

4 Strings

5 Percussion

6 Full Orchestra

46
Full Performance

Piano
PDF on
Enhanced
CD

Spin the Wheel of Color

SKILLS ASSESSED: Independent Singing; Rhythm Performance

Words and Music by
CRISTI CARY MILLER

(4-measures introduction)

Two-beat (♩ = 98)

* On the recording, there is a 2-measure interlude, then entire song repeats again.

Teaching Suggestions

To Prepare: *Gather an assortment of red, yellow, blue, and green plastic cups; one for each child. Select a cup from each colored group and mark an "X" on the inside bottom.*

1. Explain you will be clapping the first four phrases of this song (ms. 1-8). Challenge the children to identify like phrases. *(All are the same.)*
2. Write this two-measure rhythm on a board (ms. 1-2). Clap together using rhythm syllable names.
3. Teach the first half of the song using 2-measure phrases as the students echo each phrase. Sing until words and melody are secure.
4. Sing the second half of the song (ms. 9-16) for the class while holding up the appropriate colored cup mentioned.
5. Teach the second half of the song using two-measure phrases as the students echo each phrase.
6. Sing once again as you play the part of the leader and they respond as the students. Make certain this section is very secure before proceeding.
7. Have the class form a seated circle on the floor. Place a cup in front of each child.
8. Perform the following pattern while singing the first half of the song.

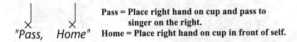

Pass = Place right hand on cup and pass to singer on the right.
Home = Place right hand on cup in front of self.

9. At the end of this section, the passing stops and all students turn their cups over to reveal the four hidden "X"s. The students holding these cups now respond to the second half of the song as the leader sings the question. *(Assessment #1)*
10. Continue singing until all have had a chance to be assessed.
11. For an added rhythm assessment, try this idea. Once the four soloists have performed, have them rotate to hand drums and play the following ostinato as the game continues. (Assessment #2)

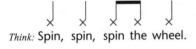

Think: Spin, spin, spin the wheel.

Assessment

Piano
PDF on
Enhanced
CD

47
Full Performance

Walkin' Down the Street

SKILLS ASSESSED: Independent Singing; Rhythm Performance

Words and Music by
CRISTI CARY MILLER

(4-measure introduction)

Moderate Shuffle (♩ = 132)

3 times *(sing 1st and 3rd times)*

While I was walk-in' down the street, (While she/he was

walk-in' down the street,) I met a brand new friend to greet. (she/he met a

brand new friend to greet.) I said, "And how do you do?" (She/he said, "And

how do you do?") "Now may I do a dance with you?" ("Now may I

do a dance with you?") So then we clapped, clapped, clapped, and then we

raised our hands up high, and then we shook each oth-er's hand and then we waved "good-bye."

OK TO
REPRODUCE

Teaching Suggestions

1. Sing the first and second Solo phrases of the song on "loo" for the students. Ask them to discuss the difference between the two phrases. *(The melodic direction of phrase one goes up and the other goes down.)*

2. Sing ms. 1-8 with the students as you perform the Solo part and they respond by singing the *Group* sections. As they reply, have them move their hands up or down on the phrase endings to show pitch direction.

3. Sing ms. 9-12 for the students. Ask them to identify the melodic direction of these four phrase **endings**. *(The melody stays on the same pitch.)*

4. Teach ms. 9-12 by rote. Ask your singers to turn to a partner and add motions to accompany each phrase, i.e. "clapped, clapped, clapped" = clap hands, etc.

5. Have the children sing through the entire song as you continue to perform the Solo sections. Switch roles and sing again.

6. When the group is comfortable with the song, direct them to make a standing circle facing outward. Select one person to walk on the outside of the circle and sing the Solo phrases with the group responding on the echoes. *(Assessment #1)* On the word "greet," the singer should stop at the closest student.

7. On ms. 9-12 only the soloist and his/her selected partner perform the dance while everyone sings.

8. After the song, the selected partner becomes the new soloist and the game continues. Play until all singers have had an opportunity to be assessed.

9. If using the full performance track (CD Track 47), the second time through the song can be used to allow time for switching soloists.

10. Add the following ostinato for an additional rhythm assessment. *(Assessment #2)*

Think: "Walk-in', walk-in',   walk down the street."

You Compose

Name _____ Class _____

Compose a Rhythm

Using any of the following notes or rests, create a rhythm that you can clap.

Your rhythm will have four beats in every measure, and a total of four measures. Create your rhythm on this single-line staff. Then clap your rhythm along with the Rhythm Track. There are two measures of a Cowbell at the beginning of the Track.

Form groups of three. Take turns listening to each person in your group clap their rhythm. Now clap these rhythms along with the Rhythm Track.

What instruments could be used to play these rhythms? Play your rhythms on those instruments along with the Track.

Compose a Melody

Create a melody using any of the following pitches.

C   D   E   F   G   A   B   C

You may use any of these notes or rests. Again, there are four beats in every measure. Your new melody should last eight measures.

Here are some helpful hints for creating your melody. There are suggested pitches written below each measure. Feel free to use these if you would like. Move smoothly from one pitch to the next so you are not making wide leaps.

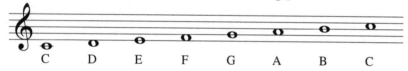

   (E - G - B)   (C - E - G - A)   (D - E - F - G)   (G - A - C)

   (E - G - B)   (C - D - E - F)   (G - A - C)   (E - G -A)

Play your melody on a pitched instrument. Play along with the Melody Track. Feel free to change pitches or rhythms to match the accompaniment. There are four clicks at beginning of the Track.

Ask two classmates to play their melodies on pitched instruments one after the other. Then play your melody followed by your two classmates' melodies. Play along with the Track.

Name _____   Class _____

INSTRUMENT WORD SEARCH

DIRECTIONS: Locate and circle the words in the word search puzzle from the list below. Look up, down, right, left, diagonally and backwards.

```
N  G  X  T  G  H  U  R  T  I  M  P  A  N  I  U  R  V  L  E
N  P  S  Y  B  A  S  S  O  O  N  R  Z  L  O  J  Q  T  Y  P
F  L  Z  Z  V  W  E  N  Q  I  Y  M  P  T  S  L  T  R  S  Z
A  W  U  A  F  F  J  F  Z  J  B  E  E  E  D  S  P  O  X  L
K  H  O  C  T  V  C  L  A  R  I  N  E  T  I  R  M  M  Y  K
D  B  R  O  F  R  G  Q  U  X  G  R  E  V  A  C  B  B  L  P
W  G  Z  Z  D  P  I  V  X  J  P  P  L  H  E  B  A  O  O  L
Q  S  E  O  O  B  P  A  X  C  M  F  U  B  B  S  S  N  P  M
G  Q  V  T  U  R  L  E  N  U  I  W  L  F  L  R  S  E  H  S
H  Z  I  A  B  N  Z  O  R  G  A  T  U  U  W  X  D  B  O  T
P  U  O  M  L  C  F  T  C  G  L  F  W  D  T  F  R  F  N  N
F  T  L  B  E  H  E  T  P  K  L  E  H  D  Z  E  U  I  E  R
N  R  A  O  B  K  I  L  Q  S  E  H  V  S  K  M  M  E  F  H
P  W  O  U  A  F  T  D  L  A  C  T  J  A  L  V  Q  C  E  K
F  N  N  R  S  J  U  M  B  O  U  F  U  Q  S  I  U  U  N  A
U  J  G  I  S  N  A  R  E  D  R  U  M  B  R  O  L  O  B  R
R  B  V  N  Q  G  Y  X  X  E  C  H  O  A  A  L  H  B  E  X
E  D  P  E  K  U  U  O  I  R  M  F  W  R  U  I  G  O  K  P
Z  X  R  I  D  T  S  H  K  W  F  E  D  J  C  N  R  E  Z  T
X  G  F  R  E  N  C  H  H  O  R  N  G  L  Q  H  L  B  V  A
```

VIOLIN	TAMBOURINE	TRUMPET	TIMPANI
VIOLA	FLUTE	FRENCH HORN	XYLOPHONE
CELLO	CLARINET	TROMBONE	SNARE DRUM
DOUBLE BASS	OBOE	TUBA	BASS DRUM
HARP	BASSOON	TRIANGLE	WOODBLOCK

The Music Year Challenge
(What have we learned?)

Name _____ Class _____

This year we did a lot of singing. We added many new songs! Write the titles of three of your favorite songs learned in music class.

1. _____

2. _____

3. _____

Rhythms were an important part of our learning this year. We studied these notes. How many beats does each note get? Fill in the blanks.

4. ____ ____ ____ ____ ____ ____ ____ ____

Add **one** note to complete each of these measures so there are four beats. Once you have completed the measures, clap the rhythms to check your work.

5.

Music Math
Complete these musical math problems.

6a. ♩ + ♩ = _____ beats

6b. 𝅗𝅥 + 𝅗𝅥 = _____ beats

6c. 𝄽 + 𝄽 + ♩ = _____ beats

6d. 𝅝 – 𝅗𝅥 = _____ beats

6e. 𝅝 + 𝄽 + 𝅗𝅥 = _____ beats

6f. 𝅝 – ♩ = _____ beats

6g. 𝄻 – 𝄽 = _____ beats

6h. 𝅝 + 𝄽 + 𝄼 = _____ beats

6i. ♩ + 𝅗𝅥 + 𝅝 = _____ beats

6j. 𝅝 + 𝅝 + 𝅗𝅥 = _____ beats

Pitches were introduced as well. We learned their letter names (C, D, E, etc.) as well as the syllables on which to sing (Do, Re, Mi, etc.).

Fill in the letter **and** syllable names of the following melody. Then sing the melody using syllables.

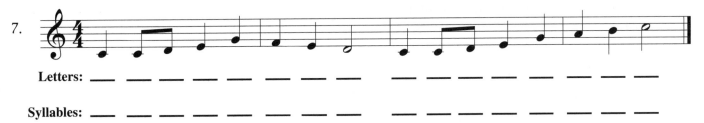

7.

Letters: __ __ __ __ __ __ __ __ __ __ __ __ __ __ __ __

Syllables: __ __ __ __ __ __ __ __ __ __ __ __ __ __ __ __

We used instruments to accompany many of our songs. Which were two or three of your favorite instruments and why were they your favorites?

8. _____

9. _____

10. _____

11. What is a partner song? _____

12. What is an ostinato? _____

13. *Fanfare for the Common Man* was written by American composer _____.

14. Benjamin Britten wrote *The Young Person's Guide to the* _____ to help introduce families of instruments to young concert goers.

Name the 4 families of instruments in the orchestra, and one instrument from each family.

15a. _____   15b. _____

16a. _____   16b. _____

17a. _____   17b. _____

18a. _____   18b. _____

Have a great summer and come back next fall ready to learn even more about music!

Page 44 · Article Worksheet – Aaron Copland

1. 1900
2. Brooklyn, NY
3. his older sister
4. Nadia Boulanger
5. steam locomotive
6. The Second Hurricane

Page 46 · Article Worksheet – Benjamin Britten

1. Saint Cecilia
2. Gloriana
3. War Requiem
4. 1961
5. Young Person's Guide Orchestra

Page 53 · Instrument Word Search

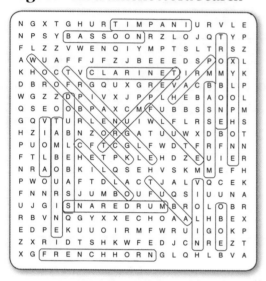

Page 54 and 55 · The Music Year Challenge

4. 1 1 2 2 3 4 4 1

5.

6. a. 2   c. 3   e. 7   g. 1   i. 7
    b. 4   d. 2   f. 3   h. 7   j. 10

7. Letters: C C D E G F E D C C D E G A B C

    Syllables: Do Do Re Mi Sol Fa Mi Re Do Do Re Mi Sol La Ti Do

11. 2 different song melodies sung together at the same time that sound good together
12. a repeated pattern
13. Aaron Copland
14. Orchestra
15. a. strings   b. violin, viola, cello, string bass
16. a. woodwinds   b. piccolo, flute, clarinet, oboe, bassoon, contra bassoon
17. a. brass   b. trumpet, French horn, trombone, tuba
18. a. percussion   b. timpani, bass drum, snare drum, triangle, tambourine, woodblock, xylophone